THE LAST SPECIES

ENDLINGS

Pinta Island Tortoise

by Joyce Markovics

CHERRY LAKE PRESS

Ann Arbor, Michigan

CHERRY LAKE PRESS

Published in the United States of America by Cherry Lake Publishing Group

Ann Arbor, Michigan

www.cherrylakepublishing.com

Reading Adviser: Beth Walker Gambro, MS Ed., Reading Consultant, Yorkville, IL

Content Adviser: David R. Sischo, PhD, Wildlife Biologist

Book Designer: Ed Morgan

Photo Credits: A. Davey/flickr, cover; Mike Weston/flickr, title page; Mike Weston/flickr, 4; Courtesy of Galapagos National Park, 5; © hytographics/Shutterstock, 6; Wikimedia Commons, 7; © nwdph/Shutterstock, 8; © Jess Kraft/Shutterstock, 9; © ChameleonsEye/Shutterstock, 10; © Andrey Bryzgalov/Shutterstock, 11; © evenfh/Shutterstock, 12; © Alejandro Martinez/Alamy Stock Photo, 13; Wikimedia Commons, 14; © Angie Ip/Shutterstock, 15 top; freepik.com, 15 bottom; © Jess Kraft/Shutterstock, 16; © Andreas Wolochow/Shutterstock, 16; Wikimedia Commons, 18; © Olga Kolos/Alamy Stock Photo, 19; © Helge Zabka/Shutterstock, 20–21; Wikimedia Commons, 22.

Cherry Lake Press is an imprint of Cherry Lake Publishing Group.

Library of Congress Cataloging-in-Publication Data

Names: Markovics, Joyce L., author.
Title: Pinta Island tortoise / by Joyce Markovics.
Description: Ann Arbor, Michigan : Cherry Lake Publishing, [2023] | Series:
   Endlings. The last species | Includes bibliographical references and
   index. | Audience: Grades 4-6
Identifiers: LCCN 2022004096 (print) | LCCN 2022004097 (ebook) | ISBN
   9781668909683 (hardcover) | ISBN 9781668911280 (paperback) | ISBN
   9781668912874 (ebook) | ISBN 9781668914465 (pdf)
Subjects: LCSH: Galapagos tortoise—Juvenile literature. | Galapagos
   tortoise—Conservation—Juvenile literature. | Endangered
   species—Juvenile literature.
Classification: LCC QL666.C584 M37 2023 (print) | LCC QL666.C584 (ebook)
   | DDC 597.92/46—dc23/eng/20220315
LC record available at https://lccn.loc.gov/2022004096
LC ebook record available at https://lccn.loc.gov/2022004097

Printed in the United States of America by
Corporate Graphics

CONTENTS

Goodbye, George

In June 2012, Lonesome George stretched his long neck for the last time. That's when Fausto Llerena found the giant Galápagos tortoise's huge, lifeless body. For four decades, Fausto had cared for George—the last of the Pinta Island tortoises.

Lonesome George was around 100 years old when he died.

4

"He always came to greet me," said Fausto about George. "I patted his head and he stretched his neck." With George's death came the loss of an entire **species** of Galápagos tortoises. Fausto had also lost a companion. "I feel like I've lost a best friend," Fausto said.

Fausto Llerena and Lonesome George

The last known animal of its kind is called an endling. Once the endling dies, the species becomes **extinct**.

Galápagos Tortoises

Tortoises, like George, are slow-moving **reptiles** that live on land. Pinta Island tortoises are one of 15 species of Galápagos tortoises. They were some of the largest tortoises in the world, reaching up to 500 pounds (227 kilograms). These giants made their home on Pinta Island. This is one of 21 islands that make up the Galápagos **archipelago**.

The Galápagos Islands are located in the Pacific Ocean off the coast of Ecuador in South America.

The tortoises from Pinta Island had saddle-shaped shells, or carapaces (KAR-uh-peys-uhs). A notch in their shells allowed them to raise their necks. That way, the tortoises could reach and munch on tall plants.

The tortoise's saddle-shaped carapace has a honeycomb structure. This reduces its weight so the tortoise can move around more easily.

Galápago means "tortoise" in Spanish. Galápagos tortoises can live to be more than 200 years old!

Pinta Island tortoises were herbivores (HUR-buh-vores). They ate grasses, leaves, flowers, and fruits. The tortoises could store water in their bodies for later use. Amazingly, they could live without water or food for up to one year! When not eating, the Pinta Island species rested up to 16 hours a day.

Galápagos tortoises especially enjoy eating cactus stems.

Tortoises once thrived on Pinta Island and the rest of the Galápagos Islands. They roamed the hilly slopes by the thousands. Starting in the 1500s, explorers and sailors arrived on the islands. They hunted the giant reptiles for food. Sometimes, they brought live tortoises onto their ships as a fresh source of meat.

The Galápagos Islands

In all, explorers and sailors killed around 200,000 Galápagos tortoises.

Humans also brought farm animals, such as goats and pigs, to the Galápagos Islands. These animals ate the same plants as the tortoises. Over time, they destroyed much of the islands' **habitats**. Some of these **non-natives** also preyed on tortoise eggs and young.

Goats will eat almost any kind of plant.

Goats introduced to Pinta Island gobbled up almost every plant, shrub, and tree there. Over the years, the goats multiplied. The few remaining Pinta Island tortoises had little to eat. As the years passed, their **population** grew smaller and smaller.

George's Journey

By the mid-1900s, most people thought Pinta Island tortoises had gone extinct. In 1971, a scientist named Joseph Vagvolgyi discovered Lonesome George by accident. Joseph was researching snails on the island when he suddenly came face to face with the big creature.

Lonesome George's Spanish name is *Solitario Jorge*. The tortoise was named after an actor.

"The tortoise was walking slowly when we first encountered him, but withdrew into his shell with a loud hiss," wrote Joseph. At the time, Joseph had no idea he had found the last Pinta Island tortoise on the planet.

When threatened, tortoises pull themselves into their shells and hiss. The hissing sound is made by the tortoise letting air out of its lungs.

Joseph told other scientists about finding Lonesome George. To protect the **rare** tortoise, they brought him to a research station on nearby Santa Cruz Island. That's where Fausto Llerena began caring for George. Every day, Fausto cleaned the big tortoise's pen, fed him vegetables, and bathed him. "I was very fond of him and would even visit him on the weekends," Fausto said.

George was brought to the Charles Darwin Research Station on Santa Cruz Island.

Fausto also took care of George when he was sick. Once, when George was moving slower than usual, Fausto figured out the tortoise had a stomachache. Fausto gave George papaya until he felt better.

Lonesome George

Papaya is a tropical fruit. It's sometimes used to soothe the stomach.

Fausto and the scientists wanted George to **mate** with other female Galápagos tortoises. Because there weren't any Pinta Island species left, any babies would be **hybrids**. However, at least there would be **offspring**.

An egg and baby Galápagos tortoise

The scientists placed several females in George's pen. George mated a couple of times. Sadly, none of the eggs hatched. "I was always hoping he would leave a **descendant**, but that was not the case," said Fausto.

George rested in a pool to stay cool in his enclosure.

Female tortoises lay tennis ball-size eggs in holes in the ground. If the eggs are healthy, they hatch after four to eight months. The hatchlings then have to dig their way out of the ground.

Saving Species

After George died, Fausto and the scientists still had hope for Galápagos tortoises. Since before George's death, they had been raising baby tortoises at the research station on Santa Cruz Island. "We have more species to protect," says Fausto. "We can't afford to give up."

Lonesome George's body was preserved. Then it was put on display at the breeding center on Santa Cruz Island.

Once hatched, the baby tortoises are cared for at the station for five years. At that age, they're big and strong enough to live on their own. Then they're released back to the islands where their **ancestors** once lived.

Galápagos tortoise hatchlings at the research station.

There are only about 10,000 to 15,000 Galápagos tortoises left in the world.

In addition to raising and releasing tortoises, people are working hard to **restore** the islands' habitats. They're removing non-native animals from the Galápagos. Thanks to these efforts, Pinta Island is now goat-free.

Recently, scientists discovered that Lonesome George may have had closer relatives than once thought. They've found Galápagos tortoises with **DNA** from the Pinta Island species. Maybe he wasn't the last Pinta Island tortoise after all.

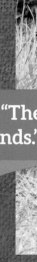

A sign at the Santa Cruz research station reads: "The fate of all living things on Earth is in human hands."

Animals Under Threat

Many more reptiles are at risk of dying out. Here are three on the brink of extinction:

Chinese Alligator

Native to China, this alligator is about half the size of an American alligator. Only around 300 remain in the wild.

Gharial

A gharial is a fish-eating crocodile with a long, thin snout that lives in India. There are fewer than 250 left in the world.

Madagascan Big-Headed Turtle

This freshwater turtle with a large head makes its home on the African island of Madagascar. Once widespread, it's now at risk of becoming extinct.

Glossary

ancestors (AN-sess-turz) relatives who lived a long time ago

archipelago (ahr-kuh-PEH-luh-goh) a large group of chain of islands

descendant (dih-SEN-duhnt) an animal that's relating to other animals that lived at an earlier time

DNA (DEE EN AY) the molecule that carries the genetic blueprint for a living thing

extinct (ek-STINGKT) when a kind of plant or animal has died out completely

habitats (HAH-buh-tats) places in the wild where animals normally live

hybrids (HYE-bruhdz) young that have been bred from two different kinds of animals

mate (MATE) to come together to have young

non-natives (non-NEY-tivz) animals that do not naturally live in a particular place

offspring (OFF-spring) an animal's young

population (pop-yuh-LAY-shuhn) the number of animals living in a place

rare (RAIR) not often seen or found

reptiles (REP-tilez) cold-blooded, egg-laying animals that have a backbone

restore (ri-STOR) to bring back or establish again

species (SPEE-sheez) certain types of animals or plants

Find Out More

Books

Hoare, Ben, and Tom Jackson. *Endangered Animals*. New York, NY: DK Children, 2010.

Riera, Lucas. *Extinct: An Illustrated Exploration of Animals That Have Disappeared*. New York, NY: Phaidon Press, 2019.

Whitfield, John. *Lost Animals*. New York, NY: Welbeck Publishing, 2020.

Websites

Galápagos Conservancy: Lonesome George
https://www.galapagos.org/about_galapagos/about-galapagos/biodiversity/lonesome-george/

Six Extinctions: An Overview of the Ends of Species
https://www.amnh.org/shelf-life/six-extinctions

World Wildlife Fund: Giant Tortoise
https://www.worldwildlife.org/species/giant-tortoise

Index

About the Author

Joyce Markovics has written hundreds of books for kids. She hopes this book inspires young reader s to learn more about endangered animals and take action to prevent their extinction. She dedicates this book to Ed, one of Lonesome George's biggest fans.